DATE DUE		
FEB 2 0 1996		
MAR 0 9 1996		
NOV 0 9 1998		
APR 2 0 1999		
MAY 2 2 2014		
APR 1 4 2015		

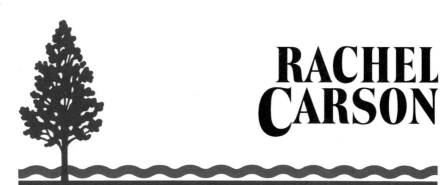

RACHEL
CARSON

Also by Eve Stwertka

PSYCHOANALYSIS: From Freud to the Age of Therapy

with Albert Stwertka
GENETIC ENGINEERING (Revised edition)

MARIJUANA (Revised edition)

PHYSICS: From Newton to the Big Bang

RACHEL CARSON

by Eve Stwertka

A FIRST BOOK
FRANKLIN WATTS
NEW YORK/LONDON/TORONTO/SYDNEY/1991

Cover photographs courtesy of: UPI/Bettmann Newsphotos (inset); Jeff Greenberg/
Tony LaGruth

Photographs courtesy of: Texas Department of Agriculture: pp. 11,
51 (both Karen Dickey); UPI/Bettmann Newsphotos: p. 13; Monkmeyer
Press Photo: pp. 16 (Paul Conklin), 54 (David Schaefer); Yale
University, Beineke Library: pp. 17, 19, 23; U.S. Fish and Wildlife
Service: pp. 28 (Rex Gary Schmidt), 43 (Patuxent Wildlife Research
Center); Rachel Carson Council Inc.: pp. 30 (Edwin Gray),
33 (Shirley Briggs), 46 (Erich Hartmann); Photo Researchers: pp. 35
(Fred McConnaughey), 39 (Bob Salmon), 53 (James T. Spencer), 55
(Tom McHugh); New York Public Library, Picture Collection: p. 41;
Augusta, Maine, Office of Tourism: p. 52; N.A.S.A.: p. 56.

Library of Congress Cataloging-in-Publication Data

Stwerka, Eve.
Rachel Carson / by Eve Stwertka.
p. cm. — (A First book)
Includes bibliographical references (p.) and index.
Summary: Describes the life and studies of Rachel Carson,
highlighting her writing and activities to save the environment.
ISBN 0-531-20020-5
1. Carson, Rachel, 1907–1964—Juvenile literature. 2. Ecologists—
United States—Biography—Juvenile literature. [1. Carson,
Rachel, 1907–1964. 2. Conservationists. 3. Biologists.]
I. Title. II. Series.
OH31.C33S79 1991
574'.092—dc20
[B]
[92]
90-13092 CIP AC

CONTENTS

RACHEL
CARSON

CHAPTER 1
THE CHALLENGER

The woman on the television screen didn't look like a fighter. She was slim, pale, dark-haired, and soft-spoken. Yet, her determination held like steel. Her name was Rachel Carson, and she had just published a shocking book. In it, she spoke up for the future of planet Earth. The year was 1962.

The book, *Silent Spring,* presented a challenge to the chemical industry, and the industry fought back. As soon as Ms. Carson's book reached the public, she was criticized and attacked. Some newspapers and magazines called her a crank, a health nut, a nervous, exaggerating woman. But Rachel Carson's scientific training had taught her to ignore personal insults. Instead, she stuck to the problem she perceived. Her weapons were facts and logical arguments. She could hold her own.

THE NEW POISONS

What started this confrontation with the chemical industry? During World War II, researchers developed a new range of chemical *pesticides,* or poisons to kill insects, weeds, and other kinds of pests. Depending on whether they were meant to destroy insects, unwanted plants, or fungus blights such as mold, the pesticides were called *insecticides, herbicides,* or *fungicides.* In general, they are sometimes referred to as *biocides* (*bio* meaning "life," and *cide* meaning "killer").

The most widely used of the new pesticides was *DDT*—short for dichlorodiphenyltrichloroethane. Chemically, it belongs to a group of compounds called *organochlorides* because they contain organic molecules and chlorine atoms.

The new chemicals did their job very efficiently.

Along with destroying insects, weeds, and other pests, insecticides and pesticides have killed numerous varieties of wildlife. This bird, killed by pesticides, is just one example of the vast damage done by the use of these chemicals.

Unfortunately, though, when they were spread on farm crops or sprayed from airplanes over woods and lakes, they killed not only pests, but also birds, fish, and other small animals. Worse than that, scientists were beginning to find out that DDT and related pesticides remained poisonous for years. Even sun, rain, bacteria, or acids in the soil hardly affect them. Deposited in nature, these chemicals enter everything that grows there—cereals, fruits, vegetables, fish, meat, and milk. Tests show that DDT remains in the body tissues of people who eat the products dusted with this pesticide, possibly causing cancer and other illnesses.

Most people using the new biocides were not aware of their devastating effects. Farmers, gardeners, storekeepers, and householders were delighted to buy such efficient pest killers. As for the manufacturers, they developed more and more of the new products, advertising them as miracle controls for everything from cockroaches to poison ivy. Soon, biocides were used by the tons. Townspeople sprayed against mosquitoes; railroad workers against weeds along the tracks; fruit growers against caterpillars. People actually

Rachel Carson stirred up a national controversy when she began writing about the harm we were doing to our environment.

thought they could destroy every disturbing weed or bug in nature.

When swarms of fish and birds died after pesticide spraying from the air, some scientists began reporting the long-lasting and harmful effects of the new poisons. But the chemical companies denied their responsibility. For several years, not even the government wanted to get involved.

ECOLOGY AND CONSERVATION

Silent Spring was an urgent warning that the new pesticides needed to be restricted and supervised. But Rachel Carson did far more than caution us against the immediate threat of these chemicals. Before any of her books were widely read, the idea of *ecology*— the study of the relationship between living organisms and their physical environment—was unfamiliar to most people. Individuals and governments gave little thought to the conservation of natural surroundings and resources.

Carson showed us that all creatures are linked together in a chain of existence. We humans are part of this chain, and before we break any links in it, we'd better plan for the consequences. After all, planet Earth is our only home. Rachel Carson's writings remind us to treat it with foresight and care.

CHAPTER 2
ON THE FARM

Rachel Louise Carson was born in Springdale, Pennsylvania, on May 27, 1907. Her parents' modest farm overlooked a bend in the Allegheny River. This was pretty countryside. But even in those days, nature was already suffering from the scars of nearby mining operations and the black smoke of industrial mills.

Rachel was the youngest of three children, born ten years after her sister, Marian, and eight years after her brother, Robert. By the time she came along, the older children were starting to be fairly independent, which left their mother free to spend time with her youngest child.

Maria Carson had been a teacher before her marriage. She delighted in showing her daughter the natural wonders all around them. Mrs. Carson taught

The lovely countryside that surrounded Carson during her childhood was marred by the effects of strip mining.

*Rachel Carson with her mother, Maria.
Mrs. Carson's love of nature was a
tremendous inspiration to her daughter.*

Rachel the names of animals, birds, and plants and pointed out small hidden forms of life among the grasses and under the bark of trees. Rachel was a delicate child, and often her mother kept her home from school. Together they talked, read, and took long walks. Young Rachel liked to write little stories and make charming drawings of animals and flowers.

Rachel's father, Robert Carson, was a businessman. Although his real estate ventures didn't prosper and he was forced to take a series of jobs, he kept the farm going as long as he could. The Carson children ate delicious crunchy apples from their orchards and had fun with the pigs, livestock, chickens, and the family horse that drew their carriage.

From earliest times, Rachel was surrounded by animals. Helping to feed and care for them, she had a chance to observe their ways. When she roamed across woods and fields, she was usually accompanied by their dog, Candy. Later in life, she would always have at least one pet—a cat or a dog, and often

This old photograph shows Rachel's parents, Robert and Maria, on a visit to Rachel at Pennsylvania College for Women in 1925.

both. During the long, hard months of work on *Silent Spring,* she enjoyed the company of Jeffie the cat, who liked to sleep curled up on the writing desk.

FIRST STEPS TO SUCCESS

In 1917, just before Rachel's tenth birthday, America entered World War I. When her brother joined the Army Aviation Service, his tales of bombs, air battles, and heroic patriotism fascinated her. Rachel wrote a story about a daring fighter pilot whose plane is shot at and crippled over Germany.

Rachel sent this story off to a children's magazine called *St. Nicholas,* and before long, "A Battle in the Clouds" by Rachel L. Carson (age ten) was published. She received a ten-dollar check in the mail.

After high school, not many young women of Rachel's generation went on to college. But Rachel was exceptionally gifted and determined to study. With her family's encouragement and the help of a scholarship, she entered Pennsylvania College for Women (later renamed Chatham College). Her major subject was to be English literature.

CHAPTER 3

THE PULL OF THE OCEAN

In her first year of college, Rachel published a story in the school magazine. Called "The Master of the Ship's Light," it takes place on the wild seacoast "where the rugged bulk of Cape Arrowhead, a queer misshapen nose of granite, juts out into the waters." Here, she tells about "patches of white foam, betraying the menacing reefs beneath," about "icy winds," "towering waves," and the "booming of breakers."

Surprisingly, the young woman who wrote these powerful descriptions had never been near the ocean. Even though she grew up far inland, the sea had always fascinated Rachel. Stories about the sea had been her favorite childhood reading.

Perhaps it seemed to her that the ocean, unlike the land, could never be spoiled, but would remain forever fresh. In the Pennsylvania countryside surrounding Rachel's home, she had seen how quickly nature could be blighted. Shipping and factory wastes had turned the clear river into a yellowish, polluted ditch. Whole wooded mountains had been *strip-mined* and transformed into gray heaps of rubble.

A CHANGE OF DIRECTION

Rachel Carson took a biology course in her second year of college with an inspiring teacher, Mary Scott Skinker, who became a good friend. Rachel loved the fun of hunting for biological specimens, the quiet concentration of the laboratory, and the wonders revealed under the microscope. By the time she graduated from college with high honors, Rachel had decided to specialize in *marine* zoology—the study of animal life in the ocean.

NO PLACE FOR A WOMAN

Shy and gentle on the surface, Rachel Carson was something of a rebel under the skin. In those days, the scientific professions were considered to be strictly for men. Only a few talented women were admitted to graduate schools. Rachel was one of them. In 1929, aquatic biologist. Eventually, this job turned into quite a career. In 1949, Rachel Carson became editor in chief for all publications of the Fish and Wildlife Service.

At the end of the first year in Rachel's new job, her supervisor was particularly struck by a piece of writing about the sea he had assigned to her. He advised her to send it to the magazine *The Atlantic Monthly*, where the article was published in September 1937. Its very title, "Undersea," indicates her fascination with the drama of life below the surface of things.

FIRST OF THE OCEAN BOOKS

Rachel's acceptance by a nationwide magazine came just in time to boost her spirits and help her finances. Some months earlier, she had been forced to take on new and heavy responsibilities. Her sister had died, leaving two teenage daughters, who now joined Rachel's household. With renewed confidence, "Ray," as her friends called her, resolved to expand "Undersea" into a longer work.

In 1941, she published the first of her famous ocean books, *Under the Sea-Wind*. In this magical work, she shows us a thrilling underwater world in continual change—exciting, dangerous, inhabited by myriad forms of life.

Ms. Carson's work initially stemmed from
her early fascination with the sea.
Here she and an associate take specimens
from a sea wall in the Florida keys.

At first, *Under the Sea-Wind* did not catch on with the public. America had just entered World War II, and people were too preoccupied with the war to spend time reading about the flight of birds and the migration of fish.

All the same, Rachel went on writing. She had an idea for a new book about the ocean, its history, and its importance to life on Earth.

SUCCESS AND FAME

Rachel's diligence was rewarded in 1951. *The Sea Around Us* appeared in bookstores and was an immediate success. World War II had ended several years before, travel and exploration had started again, and people were taking a new look at their environment.

Even before the book came out, parts of it were published in *The New Yorker, Nature Magazine,* and *Reader's Digest.* It was a Book-of-the-Month Club selection and stayed on the *New York Times's* bestseller list for eighty-one weeks. Rachel received the National Book Award for the best nonfiction book of 1951, and two colleges awarded her honorary doctorates. Since *The Sea Around Us* proved such a success, it seemed a good time to bring out a new edition of *Under the Sea-Wind.* And now, this book also rose to the bestseller list. Rachel Carson had become famous.

The invention of scuba equipment opened up new worlds for scientists like Rachel Carson. Divers could now descend to depths previously unknown to observe and study marine life.

the sea floor for two weeks, swimming in and out of the unit to study a coral reef nearby.

While all this was starting to happen, however, Rachel Carson's thoughts had already turned away from the sea, in the direction of her last and greatest project.

CHAPTER 5
DEAD SONGBIRDS

Early in 1945, Rachel's employer, the U.S. Fish and Wildlife Service, started an experimental control program with the new pesticide DDT. Rachel offered to write an article on the program for *Reader's Digest*. Her letter reads in part:

> The experiments . . . have been planned to show what effects DDT may have if applied to wide areas: what it will do to insects that are beneficial or even essential; how it may affect waterfowl, or birds that depend on insect food; whether it may upset the whole delicate balance of nature if unwisely used.

The magazine showed no interest in these urgent questions, and for the moment, Rachel was forced to drop the subject. She was busy with a series of government pamphlets, *Conservation in Action*, about national wildlife refuge areas.

A few years passed. One day, an indignant letter reached her from a friend living in Massachusetts. A mosquito-control plane had been spraying DDT over the marshes close by the friend's house. The day after the plane crisscrossed above her garden, the woman picked up three dead songbirds. The following day, four more birds lay scattered around her backyard. The day after that, she saw a robin suddenly drop from its perch on a tree.

Rachel, who loved birds and spent hours with her binoculars watching their nesting habits and flight patterns, found her worst fears confirmed. Far more was at stake, of course, than the sound of songbirds. The threat of destruction extended to all of nature, including the health and lives of humans. This marked the beginning of the landmark book to be called *Silent Spring*.

POISONS IN THE FOOD CHAIN

In one way or another, all living creatures depend on each other for food. Just about every eater eventually gets eaten. Tiny forms of sea life are eaten by small

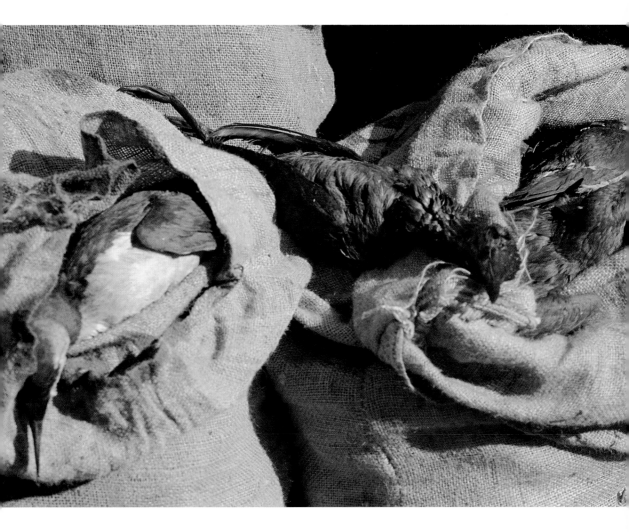

*Nature's creatures do not suffer
from the effects of pesticides only.
These dead birds are but one result
of an oil spill—another kind of
environmental disaster caused by people.*

fish, who are snapped up by bigger fish. These are devoured by a still bigger fish, and this one may eventually end up cooked on somebody's dinner plate.

Birds and insects, animals and plants—all are part of the cycle, and so are humans. This series of dietary connecting links is called the *food chain*. What affects one part of the chain affects all.

Most Americans eat high on the food chain, which isn't necessarily a good thing. Chemicals like DDT are not *soluble* in water, but they are soluble in fat. Unlike other things we eat, DDT can't be made harmless by digestion and eliminated from the body. Instead, it is stored up in the fatty tissues of animals, fish, and people, and may become highly concentrated there. When it is passed on from eater to eater, up the food chain, its concentration keeps increasing.

In addition, DDT and similar organochlorides stay toxic for years. Unlike many other poisons, they do not break down and become harmless after a few weeks. It takes ten to twenty years for DDT to be reduced to about half its quantity. DDT has been found in soil fifteen years after a single spray application.

DDT sprayed from the air later turns up in the tissues of cows and in their milk, and in the tissues of children and adults who eat dairy products. It seeps down to the groundwater, or runs into lakes and rivers. It reaches humans in fish and poultry, vegetables and fruits.

Any chemical that can destroy small organisms

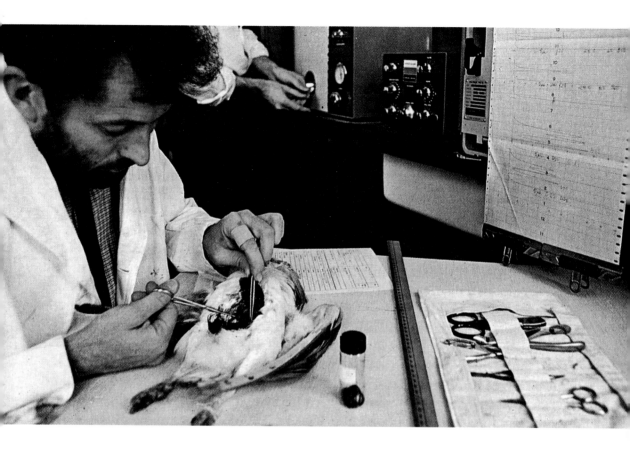

A scientist examines a dead barn owl.
It turned out that the bird's liver contained
significant quantities of residues of DDT.
The probable source of the poison
was grain, treated with pesticides, and
later eaten by mice that, in turn, were
eaten by the owl. This is an example
of how toxic residues are capable of
being passed along the food chain.

must be just as capable of damaging the cells of the human body. Strangely enough, people were slow to recognize this fact. By the time Rachel Carson started work on *Silent Spring,* however, evidence was coming in that DDT apparently caused blood disorders such as *leukemia* and other types of cancer.

Wild creatures, too, showed the ill effects of DDT. Among birds, many that survived lost the ability to produce eggshells strong enough to protect their young. Unborn birds died in the nest, and certain species became almost extinct.

THE BALANCE OF NATURE

In her writing, Rachel Carson repeatedly teaches us one basic lesson: by feeding upon each other, the numerous life forms in nature keep one another in check. Humans are part of this system. When we try to poison huge populations of pests, we upset the natural balance. As a result, we may end up destroying nature and poisoning ourselves.

To some extent, Carson tells us, nature "fights back." Not only are modern pesticides a threat to wildlife and to human health, but often they actually work against us.

For one thing, most pesticides don't kill just one particular pest, but also destroy other life in the area,

on this fragile, dedicated young woman that she never felt free enough to move away and form another bond. Rachel Carson died on April 14, 1964 at the age of fifty-six.

With the banning of organochlorides, one stage of Rachel Carson's battle for the environment ended. But new solutions also brought new problems.

Ms. Carson near her home in Maine in 1961. She was always watching and studying the life around her.

THE EARTH, TOMORROW

In many parts of the world, DDT is still legal to use. Looking back, we actually find that it had its useful side. For the first time in history, it gave humans a tool for controlling dreadful diseases such as typhoid, plague, and sleeping sickness that are largely transmitted by insects. Through the efforts of the World Health Organization, DDT saved millions of people from the risk of malaria. Those countries that still use DDT now apply it with greater care and in smaller amounts than before.

The world population keeps growing, and bigger harvests are needed than ever before. Chemical pesticides seem to be a fact of modern life. In the United States, a new group of chemicals called *organophos-*

phates has replaced organochlorides. They are preferred because they don't remain harmful very long, but they are dangerous to the people who have to handle them.

INTEGRATED PEST MANAGEMENT

Today, scientists concerned about our health and environment believe in combining many different ways to control pests. One possibility is to support natural enemies in exterminating certain pests. Another way is to release sterilized male insects so that when breeding occurs there will be no offspring. Yet another way is to simulate the scent of female insects in order to lure the males into traps. These are biological controls.

Farmers are also encouraged to plant pest-resistant strains of crops, or to change and rotate crops frequently. Ancient methods such as picking off insects by hand or stripping off diseased parts of plants are also recommended. Today this may be done with special vacuum cleaners. But the numerous workers such methods require still makes them costly. Programs like these, combined with a moderate amount of spraying, are called *integrated pest management,* or IPM.

THE CASE OF THE BOLL WEEVIL

A good example of integrated pest management is the program used by American cotton growers to contain *boll weevils,* which devour the buds and bolls of cotton plants. The boll weevil became resistant to DDT in the 1940s, after a few years of successful spraying. Disaster threatened the cotton industry, until a five-part control program was tried. Early in the spring, farmers spray lightly with chemical pesticides. In the fall, before the weevils go into their *dormant* stage, farmers spray lightly again. After the cotton is harvested, all stalks and leaves that might shelter leftover insects are destroyed. When the male insects come awake the following spring, the farmers set traps for them, baited with the scent of female weevils. The last step calls for releasing swarms of *sterile* male weevils purchased from a biological laboratory. These will mate with any remaining females, but without producing offspring.

In addition, scientists recently introduced a new virus that attacks bollworms and budworms, other pests that attack cotton. As a result, pest management has been so effective that little or no chemical spraying of cotton has been necessary.

Methods like these are complicated and expensive, but they are our hope for the future. Many growers of fruits and vegetables still drench their fields with

This is what cotton plant leaves look like when the plant has been damaged by pests. There is no question that pests need to be controlled—the dilemma is how to do this with a minimum of damage to everything else in the environment.

*We all prefer to live in a world of clean,
healthy air and water and
thriving species of animal life . . .*

. . . and not in a world like this.
Left: Soap suds being discharged into
the water by an electrical plant.
Above: Dead fish from Lake Michigan.

Taking care of the earth is the responsibility of each and every one of us.

chemicals. As world citizens, we must make it known that we don't want our drinking water contaminated, our wildlife destroyed, our body tissues filled with poisonous substances. We know that we are a link in nature's great chain of being, and many of us owe this awareness to the work of Rachel Carson.

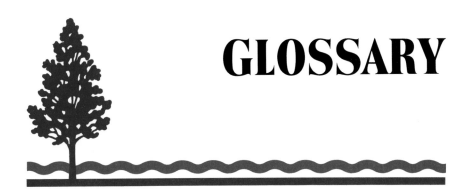

GLOSSARY

Aquatic—having to do with water

Biocide—a substance that destroys living cells (from *bio* meaning ''life'' and *cide* meaning ''killer'')

Boll weevil—an insect that attacks the cotton plant

DDT (dichlorodiphenyltrichloroethane)—a pesticide developed in the 1940s and later banned from use in the United States

Dormant—not actively growing or functioning

Ecology—the study of the interaction between living organisms and the environment

Fathom—a unit of depth measurement, equal to 6 feet (1.8 m)

Food chain—the sequence by which plants and small organisms are eaten by larger, stronger organisms, who are, in turn, eaten by still stronger organisms; the transfer of food energy through these different levels

Fungicide—a substance that destroys fungi such as mold

Herbicide—a substance that destroys plants, including weeds

Insecticide—a substance that destroys insects

Integrated pest management—an approach to pest control that stresses a combination of means and reduces the need for chemicals

Leukemia—a cancerous disease of the blood

Marine—having to do with the sea

Organochlorides—a group of chemical pesticides containing chlorine atoms attached to organic molecules; they are now banned in the United States

Organophosphates—a group of chemical pesticides containing phosphates attached to organic molecules; they are not as long-lasting in their harmful effects as organochlorides, and therefore preferred

Pesticide—a general name for a substance used to destroy any sort of invasive nuisance

Scuba—stands for *self-contained underwater breathing apparatus*; it consists of a mouthpiece joined by hoses to tanks of compressed air carried on the diver's back

Soluble—capable of being dissolved

Spider mite—an insect pest that feeds on green leaves and evergreen needles

Sterile—not capable of producing offspring

Strip mining—digging for minerals or coal in an open pit, after removing vegetation and topsoil

Underwater habitat—an artificial living unit with compressed-air supply that enables humans to spend several days underwater

Zoology—the branch of science that studies animals

FOR FURTHER READING

Brooks, Paul. *The House of Life: Rachel Carson at Work, with Selections from Her Writings Published and Unpublished.* Boston: Houghton Mifflin, 1972. Reprinted by G. K. Hall and Co., Boston, 1985

Gartner, Carol B. *Rachel Carson.* New York: Ungar Pub. Co., 1983.

Graham, Frank. *Since Silent Spring.* Boston: Houghton Mifflin, 1970.

Jezer, Marty. *Rachel Carson.* With an Introductory Essay by Matina S. Horner. New York: Chelsea House, 1988.

Marco, Gina J., Robert M. Hollingworth, and William Durham, editors. *Silent Spring Revisited*. Washington, D.C.: American Chemical Society, 1987.

Sterling, Philip. *Sea and Earth: The Life of Rachel Carson*. New York: Crowell, 1970.

For more information, write to:
Rachel Carson Council, Inc.
8940 Mill Road
Chevy Chase, MD 20815

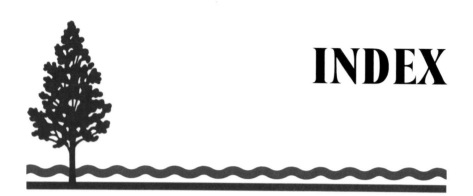

INDEX

ABOUT THE AUTHOR

Dr. Eve Stwertka has written extensively on environmental and social problems. Among her books for Franklin Watts are *Industrial Pollution, Marijuana,* and *Psychoanalysis: From Freud to the Age of Therapy.* She is Professor of English and Humanities at the State University of New York, Farmingdale.